Loaves, fishes and more...

Tasty recipes from church leaders and cooking enthusiasts

Congregational

Protecting the things you value since 1891

Contents

Credits

Edited by: Annalise Cunild, Emma Steele, Martin Edwards
Design: Paul Cocker - www.regionalmagazine.co.uk
Photography: Andy Wardle - www.detailstudios.com
Contributors: Margaret Slater, Dawn Harrison
Index by: Wendy Baskett - www.pinpointindexing.co.uk
Special thanks to: Richard Smith, Simon Webster, Pete McKee
                      Tim Treeby, Jo Spencer, Richard Shaw
                      www.relaxeatanddrink.com

First Published in   Congregational & General Insurance plc
2009 on behalf of: www.congregational.co.uk

Published by: Regional Magazine Company
                      www.regionalmagazine.co.uk

Congregational

Protecting the things you value since 1891

There's something cooking...

Acknowledgements

Congregational & General Insurance plc would like to thank the following people for their help and support in the collation of this book

Thanks must first go to **Kevin Woodford** for kindly contributing his own recipes as well as judging the submitted recipes and lending an expert eye throughout the compilation of the book.

The **members of the public** who donated recipes must be also thanked for taking the time and effort to make their contributions which will be enjoyed by so many.

We would also like to thank the following denominations for supplying a recipe:
Gillian Ashmore, Recording Clerk, Religious Society of Friends (Quakers)
www.quakers.org.uk
Revd Dr Martyn Atkins - General Secretary, Methodist Church – www.methodist.org.uk
Revd Jonathan Edwards General Secretary, Baptist Union of Great Britain
www.baptist.org.uk
Wayne Hawkins - President Elect Congregational Federation - www.congregational.org.uk
Commissioner John Matear - Territorial Commander Salvation Army –
www.salvationarmy.org.uk
Sheila Redwood - The Provincial President of the Mothers Union on behalf of The Scottish
Episcopal Church – www.scotland.anglican.org
Rev Roberta Rominger - General Secretary United Reformed Church – www.urc.org.uk
Revd Haydn Thomas - Moderator of the Presbyterian Church of Wales – www.ebcpcw.co.uk
The Most Reverend and Rt Hon the Lord Archbishop of Canterbury, **Rowan Williams** Church
of England – www.cofe.anglican.org

We are also grateful to **Gordons LLP**, Leeds, which carried out vital copyright and licensing work without which the project would not have been possible.

Thank you to **PCD Agency**, Leeds for producing the website and providing the book concepts.

The team at **The Cricket Inn**, Sheffield, have done a tremendous job cooking the recipes for photography and contributing the delicious bread recipes. Thank you to **Richard Smith, Simon Webster, Tim Treeby, Jo Spencer** and **Richard Shaw**.

Thanks also to **Andy Wardle** for photography and to **Pete Mckee** for his illustration.

Our sincere thanks go to **Lucre Public Relations**, Leeds for their help in promoting the book and bringing it to the public eye and to everyone at the **Regional Magazine Company** for the production and also Wendy Baskett for her indexing services.

Finally thanks to the **Christian Aid** team for sharing the vision.

Foreword

Congregational

Protecting the things you value since 1891

It is with a great sense of pride that we at Congregational & General Insurance bring you this very special cookbook, our unique not-for-profit fundraising initiative. Our Company has been enabling congregations to worship for over a century with the provision of specialist insurance.

We are wholly owned by the Congregational & General Charitable Trust, which actively disburses a proportion of our profits to charitable causes including churches, schools, colleges and community projects.

We are often approached by church communities and charity groups asking us to help them with their fundraising activities. In the ideal world we'd give to every request but that simply isn't feasible. This book represents our attempt to get a little closer to the ideal.

The current vogue for cooking is hard to ignore. People love trying new recipes and what better way to feed into that than by collecting well-loved recipes from members of our church communities?

Twelve months ago we approached church leaders across the UK inviting them to participate in this pioneering initiative by submitting their favourite recipe. Our goal was to help church community groups raise funds for their own cause whilst also making a donation to Christian Aid.

The decision to bring in Christian Aid was a natural one as the organisation shares our core values and is a key force in helping those people most in need. Daleep Mukarji OBE, director of Christian Aid, has lent his full support to the project and explains in the following pages why this fundraising is so important to the charity.

As recipes poured in for the book from church leaders and members of the public alike, we realised we were onto something special.

Kevin Woodford was the veritable icing on the cake; Kevin's strong faith, passion for food and shared enthusiasm for making a difference, make him the best person to lend an expert touch and we sincerely appreciate all his time, which he has given freely.

In Loaves, Fishes and More you will find a superb collection of mouth-watering recipes, some of which have been passed down through families, discovered during overseas visits or simply invented. The recipes are easy to follow, affordable dishes, which you will come back to time and time again.

One of my favourites is the Archbishop of Canterbury's ginger biscuits recipe, which I especially enjoyed making with my young daughters. I hope this cookbook gives you similar fond memories, together with the added reassurance that every purchase will mean a contribution to Christian Aid and to those church communities and charities most in need of our help.

Carlo Cavaliere
Chief Executive, Congregational & General Insurance

There's something cooking...

Kevin Woodford
An expert's opinion

Celebrity chef Kevin Woodford has shown he has the right ingredients for success. With regular television appearances on programmes such as Planet Cook and previously Ready Steady Cook, along with establishing a boutique hotel on the Isle of Man he certainly has his work cut out.

Although he's in high demand and at the top of his game, Kevin has willingly given his time to a cause he truly believes in.

"I'm constantly inundated with requests to support fundraising efforts but I have to be selective," said Kevin.

"It is not something I enter into lightly, but this is a fantastic way for local church communities and charity groups to raise money for their own causes while making a donation to Christian Aid."

Kevin was given the difficult task of selecting recipes to include in the book from the hundreds submitted by members of the public.

"I was looking for originality, best use of ingredients, variation and functionality – the recipes really needed to work."

"It was a tough process because I was trying to select a balance of recipes that would sit well in the book alongside those given to us by Church leaders."

With recipes coming from amateur cooks rather than professional chefs, Kevin needed to use his expertise to make the selections.

"They are all lovely recipes," he said. "It is great that people have taken the time and trouble to submit and share them."

"The recipes I've included are some of my favourites; they have all been tried and tested and work beautifully well. I have adapted them for this book so they are truly unique.

"They are all dishes I would want to make at home – and the Raspberry Millefeuille is to die for!"

As well as being a committed Christian, Kevin has a strong belief in the value of nutritious food and as he was growing up it was an important element in his family life.

"My mother believed good ingredients were key to a great meal and this gave me a really good start in my cooking career."

There's something cooking...

With high standards and an aspiration to become a top international chef, he was dedicated to his end goal.

"I was brought up to believe that if you do something you should do it well and to the best of your abilities so that is what I have always aimed for."

From the kitchen, Kevin moved into academia and spent several years lecturing at one of the UK's leading establishments for food technology .

"I loved the process of lecturing and communication, I enjoyed passing on my knowledge and watching people develop – it's something I miss doing."

Kevin moved from teaching students in a lecture hall to 'front of a camera' educating people in their own homes via his television career.

"I love doing live shows because it takes me back to my lecturing days.

"I didn't choose a life in the media but I don't regret any of it. I am truly blessed to have such a fascinating career."

Kevin's latest show, Planet Cook, is aimed at a younger audience and seeks to get them excited about food and healthy eating through cooking.

"It really shows the value of preparing and eating good food. The younger people learn about it the better; everyone should be able to cook there is no question about that.

There's something cooking...

"Food is central to life; it is not just about being healthy it is also a very social thing."

Tracing his life and career which is shaped around food, Kevin can look back on a lifetime of achievement.

"There have been several defining moments in my life; featuring on "This is Your Life" was a great honour and came as quite a shock. I also led a team of British chefs cooking for the President of France, which was a real privilege.

"I'm also extremely proud of having my recipes printed on the Isle of Man stamps a few years ago. They are the only stamps in the EU to depict recipes which makes them particularly special."

But it is Kevin's faith that has remained a particularly constant force in his life.

"It is good to know I have all the help I need in dealing with situations where I am under pressure, whether it is on television, in the kitchen or even having a game of golf!

"Living my life with Christian principles means I can get through these moments without imposing my problems on anyone else."

But Kevin acknowledges there are thousands of people who face greater challenges than any of us can imagine.

"It's a big old world and there are many people in need of our help and support. This is a valuable book that will bring nourishment in more ways than one."

Raspberry Millefeuille

Ingredients – Serves 6

for the biscuits:

100g unsalted butter

50g caster sugar

150g plain flour, sifted

for the millefeuille:

1 large punnet of raspberries, washed and dried

250ml double cream

1 tsp Madagascan vanilla extract

50g caster sugar

icing sugar for dusting

Method

1. Make the biscuits by creaming together the butter and caster sugar until soft and fluffy.

2. Add the flour gradually and gently knead until it forms a smooth ball. Wrap in clingfilm and chill for at least an hour. Set the oven to 150°C/300°F/gas mark 2.

3. Roll the dough to approximately 1cm thickness using a 5cm ring cutter. Place onto a lightly greased baking tray. Cook for about 30 minutes until lightly brown.

4. Remove from the oven and allow to cool. Once cold, the biscuits can be stored in an airtight container until required.

5. To complete the pudding, add the sugar and vanilla extract to the cream and lightly whip until the cream can stand in peaks.

6. Using a palette knife, cover one side of a biscuit with the cream. Place onto a plate and top with some of the raspberries. Repeat with another biscuit and place this on top of the raspberries on the first biscuit. Top this with raspberries and repeat the process once more.

7. Dust the top with icing sugar and serve.

There's something cooking...

Congregational
Protecting the things you value since 1891

Homemade shortbread
biscuits, local raspberries
and vanilla cream,
oooooooooh heaven.

Pea and Lemon Thyme Soup with Chilli Oil

This has to be simply the best soup in the world. It takes about 10 minutes to make, is really inexpensive and full of flavour. The recipe uses frozen peas, and there is a very good reason for that. They are available all year round and providing you buy good quality ones then you are guaranteed great flavour and lots of nutritional goodness for all the family. Serve piping hot with chunks of crusty bread.

Ingredients - Serves 6

10ml olive oil

25g butter

100g chopped onion

2 cloves of garlic, peeled and crushed

2 slices of streaky bacon, chopped

small handful of picked lemon thyme

1 tsp dried chillies

1 medium size bag of best quality frozen peas (petits pois)

1 litre vegetable or chicken stock

Maldon sea salt

small tub of crème fraîche

1 tbsp chilli oil

Method

1. Heat the oil and the butter in a saucepan.
2. Add the onion, garlic, bacon and cook for 5 minutes.
3. Add the lemon thyme, chillies and frozen peas, cook for a further 5 minutes and then add the chicken stock.
4. Season with the salt and bring to the boil, reduce to a simmer and cook for 10 minutes.
5. Blend the soup with a hand blender.
6. Serve topped with a little crème fraîche and a swirl of chilli oil.

Kevin Woodford's Spicy Lamb Shank

Ingredients

olive oil

150g onions, diced and peeled

6 cloves of garlic, peeled and smashed

6 red chillies, seeds discarded and chillies diced

150g celery, diced

150g, leeks, diced

1tsp cumin

1tsp dried coriander

4 lamb shanks

pinch of turmeric

pinch of paprika

4 apples, peeled and diced

150g dried prunes

6 large tomatoes, skinned and diced

3tbsp sun-dried tomato puree

½ bottle of red wine

750ml lamb stock, if not available then chicken stock

salt and pepper

Method

1. Heat the olive oil in an ovenproof casserole dish. Add the onions, garlic, red chillies, celery and leeks and cook until soft.
2. Meanwhile, mix together the cumin, dried coriander, turmeric and paprika and rub it over the lamb shanks.
3. Heat a little oil in a frying pan and seal the shanks on all sides until golden brown.
4. Place the shanks into the casserole dish, add the tomatoes, apples, prunes and tomato purée, and pour on the wine and stock.
5. Season lightly with a little salt and freshly ground black pepper. Cover with a tight fitting lid and cook in a moderate oven for about 80 minutes until tender.
6. Remove the shanks from the dish and cover to keep hot.
7. Place the casserole with the sauce onto a high heat and reduce the liquid until it reaches a sauce consistency.
8. Serve the shanks on a heap of creamy mash potato and pour over the sauce.

Kevin Woodford's Simnel Cake

Ingredients

100g glace cherries

100g stem ginger

100g dried apricots

175g unsalted softened butter

175g light brown sugar

3tbsp milk

3 large eggs

175g self raising flour

25g ground almonds

100g sultanas

½ tsp grated nutmeg

1tsp ground ginger

2tsp mixed spice

500g almond paste

4tbsp apricot jam, heated

1 medium egg, beaten

Method

1. Grease and line the sides and bottom of a 20cm deep round cake tin with baking paper.
2. Chop the cherries, ginger and apricots into small pieces and place into a large bowl with all of the other ingredients with the exception of the almond paste, apricot jam and medium egg.
3. Beat until the mixture is well blended and place half the cake mix into the cake tin.
4. Roll out one third of the almond paste into a round the same size as the cake tin and place on top of the mixture. Place the remaining cake mix on top and smooth the surface.
5. Cook in a pre-heated oven at 160ºC/320ºF/gas mark 3 between 90 minutes to 2 hours until golden brown. It's often advisable to cover the top of the cake with baking foil for the last 10 minutes to prevent it gaining too much colour.
6. Leave to cool a little and then carefully turn out onto a wire rack and allow to cool.
7. Roll out the remainder of the almond paste to fit the top of the cake. Brush the surface of the cake with a little of the heated apricot jam and place this on top of the cake.
8. Using a fork crimp the edges of the cake and pattern the centre of the cake to your own design.
9. Brush the surface of the almond paste with the beaten egg and glaze under a hot grill until golden brown.

Village women in Burkina Faso bring rocks to build low walls that help to protect the soil from erosion by rain and wind. The walls also encourage rainwater to penetrate the soil, helping crops to thrive. **Photo: Christian Aid/Kevin Leighton**

A Message of Support

Fundraising is vital to Christian Aid and without the generous giving of time, money and ideas by organisations and individuals we would not be the wide-reaching charity we are today.

This book's central message of nourishment and sharing is made doubly pertinent by the support it will give to our many causes.

Food shortage is a major problem and one that we see much of through our work in the world's most impoverished countries. This is a crisis of man's making, not nature's. In 2008, according to the Food and Agriculture Organisation of the United Nations, there was enough food grown to meet the nutritional needs of every person on the planet, yet malnourishment is causing tens of thousands of deaths every day.

In the simple act of buying this book, you are helping us to take one step closer to a long-term solution to food shortage as well as bringing immediate relief to people in need.

We would like to offer our sincere thanks, not only to Congregational & General Insurance for being the driving force behind this project, but also to all the Church leaders and the people who have given up their time to share such wonderful recipes.

This is a book to be cherished; it speaks to us all not only about the joy that can come from sharing food with our friends and loved ones, but also more profoundly about the importance of giving.

Bon appetit!

Daleep Mukarji, OBE (pictured top right)
Director of Christian Aid

One project in Burkina Faso supplies farmers with livestock. Once the animals breed, the farmers hand one back to the project.
Photo: Christian Aid/Abbie Trayler-Smith

There's something cooking...

Watering onions at a women's market gardening project in Burkina Faso. Crops grown for sale locally include onions, potatoes and tomatoes. Income helps to support basic family needs such as children's clothes. **Photo: Christian Aid/Kevin Leighton**

In India, some schools are involved in teaching good farming practice, such as at this one near Hyderabad where the school garden acts as the classroom for such lessons. **Photo: Christian Aid/Kim Naylor**

Christian Aid and the Global Food Crisis

The biggest issue facing the world is not an overall shortage of food but a flawed global food system that is vulnerable to external shocks. There are already more than 800 million malnourished people in the world and more than 20,000 deaths taking place each day from hunger-related causes. With rocketing food prices pushing another 100 million people into poverty, something urgently needs to be done.

The food crisis is a man-made problem not one of nature alone. As ever, it is the poorest in the world who are being hit the hardest. Many do not grow enough food for their own needs. Instead, they grow large volumes of cash crops (such as tobacco or biofuels) for export, while importing food for their own people. This creates a shortage of staple foods in many countries. By investing equally in staple-crop production the risks of food shortages will reduce and prospects for development improve.

The worst hit by such policies are small-scale subsistence farmers (those who grow only enough to feed their family). Some have been driven off their land and denied access to resources such as water. Roughly 65% of the population relies on subsistence farming, with no fertiliser, no high-yield seeds, no irrigation and no medication for their livestock. It is vital to ensure that poor women and men can feed themselves and their families. The proportion of women in agricultural production is as high as 70% in some countries, and this group particularly suffers from deteriorating health and work conditions. This dismal situation calls for major changes.

Long-term under investment in food production has led to weakened domestic farming sectors and countries that are over-dependent on food imports. Many farmers are not in a position to respond to growing shortages when the supply of subsidised food from richer countries stops.

In recent years, droughts and other extreme weather events have hit some of the world's main grain-exporting countries hard. Therefore climate resilience and diversifying food production needs to come into play.

Population growth is partly to blame for the inability of poor countries to feed themselves. Africa is one of the worst hit by the current food shortages, with 21 countries in crisis and requiring outside aid. The continent's population almost doubled between 1975 and 2000 to 794 million, and is expected to show a similar increase by 2030. Even in countries that do grow sufficient food, consumers are facing higher prices once other factors such as rising transport costs come into force.

To find out more about Christian Aid and how you can help, visit the website at www.christianaid.org.uk

Our Daily Bread

B read has an important role in our lives as well as our beliefs. All over the world you will find different types, each with its own culture and history. Something so simple, pure and honest, is without a doubt a gift from God.

As a chef, restaurateur and keen baker I love the artisan craft of making fresh bread on a daily basis for my customers' pleasure. The joy of working with your dough, the proving, the baking, it is so simple to do. It will fill your home with a beautiful aroma and its enjoyment is second to none.

Remember, great bread isn't just baked by master bakers. It can be made successfully at home, in domestic ovens or bread makers. As with any baking though, practice makes perfect.

For me, bread takes on many forms. The smell and the taste is pure heaven, and what has always amazed me is the diversity of flavours and textures which can be created. With a similar construction of flour, water and yeast, it can deliver very different end results and deep, complex flavours. It really is truly wondrous.

From rye to rice, malt soft milled to pure white and organic to stone-ground; the various flavours from amazing mills across the world, along with wild yeasts and cultivated yeasts, create unique flavours. The nuts, herbs, seeds, cheeses, spices, purées and fruits which can be added make it so diverse, so creative.

Good bread is a beautiful thing and a treat to enjoy at any time. The honesty of the product I never ever tire of. It excites me every day and it is the stuff of life, a wondrous gift. No meal should begin without bread. Give us our daily bread please!

There's something cooking…

Hints and Tips

If the bread rises too much:
Usually caused by too much yeast – reduce by 25%.
Too much sugar will promote yeast action.
Too much liquid can sometimes cause a loaf to over rise.
A hot day, can have the same effect.
Less or no salt can cause the yeast to be uncontrolled.

Crumbly or coarse texture:
Bread rose too much.
Dough didn't have enough liquid.
Too many wholegrains were added which soak up the liquid.

If the bread does not rise enough:
Insufficient yeast or yeast that has passed its expiry date.
You rushed it, giving the bread less time to rise.
The yeast and salt came into contact with each other before mixing.
Too much salt inhibits the action of the yeast.

Knock Back
Is a term used when the chef sharply jabs the dough with their fist to release some of the air.

Proving
To 'prove' the dough cover with a clean damp tea towel and leave in a warm place for a period of time.

Richard Smith… is an award-winning chef and owner of restaurants in the North of England, including the acclaimed Artisan and Thyme Café in Sheffield.
We thank him for the use of his kitchens and for helping out with a little know-how!

Rosemary and Garlic Foccacia

These loaves are best served warm.

Ingredients

for the bread:

45ml extra virgin olive oil

20g fresh yeast

350ml luke warm water

500g white bread flour

10g salt

for the topping:

60ml extra virgin olive oil

1 bulb of roasted garlic

chopped rosemary

Method

1. Lightly oil two 25cm shallow round pizza pans.
2. Cream the yeast with 60ml water, then stir in remaining water and oil.
3. Sift the flour and salt together.
4. Make a well in the centre. Pour yeast mixture into the well and mix to a soft dough.
5. Turn dough out onto a lightly floured surface and kneed for 8-10 minutes until smooth.
6. Place into an oiled bowl and cover and leave to prove for 1-1 hour 30 minutes until doubled in size.
7. Knock back and turn out on a floured surface. Gently knead in the rosemary.
8. Divide the dough into two equal pieces and put into pans and cover. Prove for 30 minutes.
9. Uncover. Using your fingers, poke the dough to make deep dimples.
10. Drizzle over the olive oil and evenly sprinkle the garlic over each foccaccia.
11. Bake for 25-30 minutes in a 200°C/400°F/gas mark 6 oven.

Enriched Bread

Ingredients

600g strong white flour

3tbsp salt

20g fresh yeast

1tsp sugar

500ml milk

60g soft butter

2 large eggs

Method

1. Sift the flour and salt into a bowl, and make a well in the centre. Add the yeast and sugar.
2. Warm the milk and the butter.
3. Mix the milk mix into the eggs.
4. Add milk mix and knead to a smooth soft dough.
5. Put dough into an oiled bowl and cover.
6. Leave to prove for 1 hour.
7. Knock the dough back.
8. Shape into loaves.
9. Prove for about 30 minutes.
10. Eggwash prior to baking.
11. Bake at 180°C/350°F/gas mark 4 for 30 minutes.

Granary and Black Treacle Bread

Ingredients

500g granary flour

500g strong white flour

20g salt

8tbsp black treacle

20g fresh yeast

600ml luke warm water

Method

1. In a bowl mix the flours, salt and treacle.
2. Cream the yeast into the water.
3. Mix the water into the flours, little by little, just using what you need.
4. Knead the dough into a lightly-oiled bowl and cover.
5. Prove for 1-1 hour 30 minutes or until doubled in size.
6. Knock back and shape into loaves.
7. Prove for 30 minutes or until doubled in size.
8. Bake at 200°C/400°F/gas mark 6 for 30 minutes or until a nice crust has formed.

Soda Bread

Ingredients

300g soft wheat flour

50g oats

20g butter, soft

1 tbsp bicarbonate of soda

200g buttermilk/yoghurt

200g milk

50g black treacle

10g salt

Method

1. Mix everything together into a wet batter/dough.
2. Pour into two greased loaf tins 23 x 13cm and cover with foil.
3. Bake for 10 minutes at 190°C/375°F/gas mark 5 then remove the foil and bake for a further 10 minutes.
4. Remove from tins and cool on a wire rack.

Congregational

Protecting the things you value since 1891

There's something cooking...

Luscious Light Bites
...and other starters

Apple and Leek Soup

Ingredients – Serves 4

6 medium cooking apples

3 – 4 leeks

1 large onion

1 litre chicken or vegetable stock

300ml single cream or
natural yoghurt

Stilton cheese

salt and pepper

Method

1. Slice the apples, leeks and onion.
2. Cover with the stock.
3. Cook until soft and liquidize.
4. Add cream (or yoghurt) and season to taste.
5. Serve hot and for a rich finish top with crumbled Stilton cheese.

Why not try a pinch of cinnamon with this dish – it brings out the apple flavour.

There's something cooking...

Reverend Roberta Rominger, General Secretary, United Reformed Church

Pakoras with Mint Yoghurt Dip

Ingredients – Serves 2

for the mint yoghurt dip:

150g natural yoghurt

1 tbsp mint sauce

½ tbsp chilli powder

for the pakoras:

125g gram flour

1 tsp salt

½ tsp chilli powder

½ tsp ground coriander

150ml cold water

1 tbsp fresh coriander, chopped

handful of baby spinach leaves, chopped

100g mushrooms, chopped

1 tbsp oil

1 onion

Method

1. Mix the ingredients for the dip together and set aside.
2. Put the flour, salt, chilli and ground coriander in a bowl. Add enough water to make a thick batter and whisk until smooth. Leave to stand for 30 minutes.
3. Add fresh coriander to the batter and mix. Combine the spinach and mushrooms.
4. Coat the mushrooms and spinach in batter and fry until golden.
5. Chop the onion and add to the remaining batter. Form small balls of onion mixture and fry. Serve hot with dip.

Dawn Harrison, Kettering

Why not try using other vegetables?

Bake It and Fill It

Ingredients – Serves 4

4 large baking potatoes

2tbsp olive oil

4 rashers back bacon, grilled

200g goat's cheese

60g sweetcorn

half a red onion

chopped fresh parsley

salt and pepper

Method

1. Place the potatoes on a baking sheet and lightly brush with olive oil. Season well with salt and pepper.
2. Bake in a pre-heated oven at 200ºC/400ºF/gas mark 6 for approximately 1 hour until the potato is cooked through.
3. Allow to cool slightly then cut off the tops of the baked potatoes and scoop out half the flesh.
4. Meanwhile finely chop the cooked bacon rashers and slice the goat's cheese into thin rounds.
5. Finely slice the red onion and gently fry until softened and golden brown.
6. Mix in the bacon, goat's cheese, sweetcorn and fried red onion with the previously removed potato. Place back into the potato skins and grill for a few minutes until golden.
7. Sprinkle over the parsley and serve. Alternatively add your own toppings.

Squash and Potato Gratin

Ingredients – Serves 6

large knob of butter

1 large onion

1 tbsp sage, finely chopped

570ml double cream

200ml full fat milk

500g butternut squash

500g waxy potatoes such as Maris Piper, or Charlotte

50g breadcrumbs

salt and pepper

Method

1. Preheat oven to 190°C/375°F/gas mark 5.
2. Grease a gratin dish (30 x 20cm) with a little butter.
3. Melt remaining butter in a frying pan and fry the onion until soft and golden.
4. Stir in the sage and heat the cream and milk until just below boiling, then set aside.
5. Peel and deseed the squash and cut into 3mm slices. Do the same with potatoes and toss together.
6. Layer the squash and potatoes in the dish, adding a little sage, onion, salt and pepper every few layers.
7. Keep the layers flat, then pour over the cream (it should almost fully cover the vegetables).
8. Sprinkle with breadcrumbs and bake until golden brown on top for approximately 1 hour.

Donna Smith, Peterborough

There's something cooking...

Hot Piri-Piri Jumbo Prawns

Ingredients – Serves 4

Piri-Piri sauce

400g fresh jumbo prawns

olive oil

4 cloves of garlic, chopped

aioli

brown bread

black pepper

Method

1. Shake the bottle of Piri-Piri sauce thoroughly and pour desired amount over the prawns. Toss until coated.
2. Heat oil in a large frying pan, sauté the chopped garlic, when soft add the marinated prawns.
3. Cook over a high heat for 3-4 minutes, until the shells of the prawns turn pink.
4. Remove the prawns from the frying pan and pour over any excess juices.
5. Serve with aioli dip and thick crusty brown bread and season well with black pepper.

There's something cooking...

Bernard Hopkins, Telford

Spicy Chicken Wings

Ingredients – Serves 4

8 chicken wings

5tbsp Piri-Piri sauce

olive oil

black pepper

Method

1. Cut the chicken wings in half and place into a shallow dish.

2. Drizzle with olive oil and season well with black pepper

3. Pour the Piri-Piri sauce over the chicken.

4. Leave to marinate for 1 hour.

5. Place a rack in a baking tray and line the marinated wings in a single layer.

6. Cook in a preheated oven at 200°C/400°F/gas mark 6 for 40 minutes until well browned.

7. Remove the chicken from the rack and serve with a salad and a dip of your choice.

Bernard Hopkins, Telford

There's something cooking...

Sausage Supper

Ingredients – Serves 2

200g chipolata sausages

100g streaky bacon

100g onions

150g long grain rice

100g mushrooms

1 small tin of pimentos

¾ pint of stock

salt and pepper

Mrs J Calvert, Shipley

Method

1. Prick the sausages and cut them in half.
2. Fry gently over a low heat for about 2 minutes.
3. Remove the bacon rind and cut the bacon into pieces.
4. Add to the sausages and fry together for another 2 minutes.
5. Peel and slice the onions. When the sausages and bacon are starting to brown stir in the onions and rice.
6. Continue stirring the mixture over the heat until the rice has absorbed all the fat.
7. Wipe and slice the mushrooms, drain and slice the pimentos, then stir both ingredients into the pan with the stock and plenty of salt and pepper.
8. Cover the pan and simmer the mixture, stirring it occasionally for about fifteen minutes until the rice is tender and all the stock has been absorbed.
9. Check for seasoning and serve with sliced tomatoes.

Storeroom Pizza

Ingredients – Serves 2

mini or full sized pitta or naan bread

2tbsp tomato puree or tomato ketchup

oregano or basil, fresh or dried

handful of grated cheese

Method

1. Spread the tomato puree or tomato ketchup over the pitta or naan and sprinkle with herbs.
2. Top with grated cheese or any other toppings you have in your fridge.
3. Bake in a pre-heated oven at 200°C/400°F/gas mark 6 for 5-10 minutes.

There's something cooking...

Melissa Geddes, London

Sausage Plait

Ingredients – Serves 6

1 onion

oil

100g cheddar cheese

1tsp chilli powder, optional

3tbsp tomato puree

400g Lincolnshire sausage meat

1 packet puff pastry

1 egg

Method

1. Fry the onion lightly in oil and grate the cheese.
2. Place the onion, chilli powder, cheese, tomato purée and sausage meat in a bowl and mix together.
3. Roll out the pastry into an oblong shape approximately 30 x 40cm.
4. Place the mixture into the centre.
5. Plait the pastry, by placing thin strips over the filling to form a lid. (See photo).
6. Brush with beaten egg and cook at 180°C/350°F/gas mark 4 for 45 minutes or until cooked.
7. Slice to serve.

Marie Parkhill, Boston

There's something cooking...

Salmon fishcakes with Chilli

Ingredients – Serves 4

300g potatoes, peeled and diced

600g tinned wild salmon

juice of half a lemon

1 tsp dried chilli flakes or 1 fresh chilli, finely chopped

fresh coriander, roughly chopped

1 tbsp nam pla (fish sauce)

1 large egg

plain flour

olive oil

lemon wedges

salt and pepper

Method

1. Boil potatoes until tender to the point of a knife (about 20 minutes). Drain the potatoes and allow to steam in the hot pan for a minute or two. Mash finely, without adding any butter or milk.

2. Drain the salmon and put in a mixing bowl. Break up very roughly with a fork. Add the mashed potato, the juice of half a lemon, the chilli, chopped coriander and nam pla. Season to taste.

3. Mix to combine all the ingredients.

4. Chill in the fridge for half an hour.

5. Beat the egg in a wide flat bowl and cover the base of another wide, flat bowl with the plain flour.

6. Heat enough olive oil to cover the base in a non-stick frying pan to medium temperature.

7. Form the fishcake mixture into patties about 7 x 2cm.

8. Dip each one into the egg mixture and then coat in the flour. Fry in small batches until crispy, for about five minutes on each side. Serve with lemon wedges and purple sprouting broccoli on the side.

There's something cooking...

Sam Wood, Newcastle

Goat's Cheese and Caramelised Onion Crostini

Ingredients – Serves 4

1 large white onion

olive oil

1 tbsp brown sugar

1 french stick

1 clove of garlic

250g goat's cheese

sea salt

black pepper

for the optional pea purée

300g fresh or frozen garden peas

handful fresh mint leaves

Method

1. Preheat the oven to 180°C/350°F/gas mark 4.

2. Peel the onion, cut in half and slice thinly. Heat 2 tablespoons of olive oil in a saucepan and add the onion. Add a good pinch of sea salt to ensure the onions don't burn and fry on a gentle heat. Add brown sugar and black pepper and continue to fry on a gentle heat until the onion is very soft and golden. This will take at least 15-20 minutes.

3. Slice the french stick and place slices on a baking sheet. Place in the oven for 5 minutes until slightly crisp. Turn over and cook for a further 5 minutes.

4. Peel the garlic clove and rub the garlic over the slices of bread. Drizzle with olive oil and place a small amount of caramelised onions on each piece followed by a slice of goat's cheese.

5. Bake in the oven until the cheese has melted.

6. For a summer flavour serve with a pea purée by adding the peas and mint to 600ml boiling water and simmering for 5 minutes, drain the peas and mint and purée with a hand blender.

Liz Byrne, Bingley

Cheese and Potato Pie

Ingredients – Serves 6

600g potatoes, sliced

1 – 2 onions, chopped

1 leek, sliced (optional)

150 – 200g strong mature cheddar cheese, grated

250ml milk

1 tbsp cornflour

50g butter

parmesan cheese, (optional)

salt and pepper

You can also add any leftover vegetables to the dish.

Method

1. Boil the potatoes and place in a large oven dish (approximately 26cm).
2. Fry the onions and leek and add to the potatoes.
3. Stir the potatoes, onions and leek together, adding the grated cheese.
4. Place the milk in a jug with cornflour, butter and seasoning and whisk. Pour in a saucepan and stir until thickened.
5. Add the sauce to the potato mixture and smooth with a fork.
6. Grate parmesan cheese on the top (or more cheddar).
7. Cook at 200°C/400°F/gas mark 6 for 25 minutes until brown and bubbling on the top.

Congregational

Protecting the things you value since 1891

There's something cooking...

Stephanie Monaghan, Middlesex

Quick Bacon and Pea Risotto

Ingredients – Serves 4

2 shallots or 1 onion

2tbsp olive oil

25g butter

6 rashers smoked bacon, chopped

300g risotto rice

1 litre vegetable stock

100g frozen peas

50g parmesan cheese, grated

salt and pepper

Method

1. Finely chop the onion or shallots. Heat 2 tablespoons of olive oil and a knob of butter in a pan, add the onions and fry until lightly browned

2. Add the bacon and fry until it starts to crisp.

3. Add the rice and cook for a couple of minutes until it has absorbed all of the moisture in the pan. Add one ladle of stock – stir well. Keep adding a ladle of stock and stirring well until the liquid has been absorbed and the rice is tender.

4. When the rice is almost done, stir in the peas, add a little salt and pepper and cook for a further 3 minutes, until the peas are cooked.

5. Stir in a knob of butter and some freshly-grated parmesan to finish.

6. Serve with some more grated parmesan on top, season with salt and pepper and add a rocket salad on the side.

Louise Woodward, Sheffield

There's something cooking...

Pepper's Pesto Pasta

Ingredients – Serves 4

2tbsp olive oil

boiling water, enough to fill large saucepan

400g pasta of your choice

handful of pine nuts

2 peppers, any colour and chopped into thin slices

2 onions, chopped into thin slices

200g fresh green beans (optional)

1 chorizo sausage, approximately 30 narrow thin slices

4tbsp crème fraîche

2tbsp pesto (red or green)

parmesan for serving

salt

Method

1. Add 1 tablespoon of olive oil and salt to the water, then cook pasta until tender.

2. In a frying pan, lightly toast the pine nuts, tossing gently until browned. Remove from the heat and add the remaining olive oil. Once the oil is hot, add the chopped peppers, onions and green beans and cook until soft. Add the chorizo and mix in, then simmer.

3. Once the pasta is cooked, drain and add in the pepper, onion and chorizo mixture. Add the crème fraîche and pesto and mix well. Finally, add the toasted pine nuts and serve with parmesan.

Congregational

Protecting the things you value since 1891

There's something cooking...

Katie Bretherick, Leeds

Sun-dried Tomato and Walnut Pasta Salad

Ingredients – Serves 2

150g wholemeal pasta shapes

10 large sun-dried tomatoes, chopped into small pieces

½ bag of rocket and watercress salad

2tbsp walnuts, chopped

1 apple, sliced

2tbsp low fat natural yoghurt or crème fraîche

black pepper

Method

1. Cook the pasta according to packet instructions. Drain once cooked.

2. Add the sun-dried tomatoes, salad, walnuts and apple and toss the combined ingredients.

3. Stir in the yoghurt/crème fraîche thoroughly, alternatively use a light vinegrette.

4. Season with black pepper to taste.

5. Serve warm, or refrigerate for 45 minutes and serve as a cold pasta salad.

Hannah Ferguson, Richmond

Home-style Mushroom Pasta

Ingredients – Serves 2

knob of butter

1 red chilli, de-seeded and diced

100g mushrooms, sliced

3 medium tomatoes, halved

1 clove of garlic, crushed

200g pasta

1 lemon

50g parmesan

handful of flat leaf parsley, chopped

Method

1. Melt the butter in a pan, add the chilli, mushrooms and crushed garlic and tomatoes. Sauté until the mushrooms are cooked.
2. Boil the pasta in a separate pan for 10 minutes.
3. Add the cooked pasta to the mushroom mix along with the juice and zest of a whole lemon.
4. Finish with a handful of parmesan and parsley, serve with crusty bread.

Congregational

Protecting the things you value since 1891

Five-Step Chicken Satay

Ingredients – Serves 4

for the marinade:

3tbsp soy sauce

juice of 1 lime, or equivalent from bottle

1tbsp honey

garlic clove, crushed

grated ginger, approximately 1 inch or 1tsp of powered ginger

4 chicken breasts, cut to bite size strips/chunks

for the dipping sauce:

4tbsp crunchy peanut butter

6tbsp milk

Method

1. Mix the marinade ingredients and put in a bowl with the chicken pieces. Leave in the fridge for 1 hour.
2. Remove the chicken from the marinade and thread onto pre-soaked wooden skewers.
3. Grill until cooked, turning once (approximately 12 minutes).
4. In the meantime, boil the remaining marinade for a couple of minutes in a small saucepan. Mix the peanut butter and milk together and add to the saucepan to warm through. Place the mixture in a bowl to use as a dipping sauce.
5. Serve with rice or noodles.

Melissa Geddes, Balham

There's something cooking...

Spinach and Red Pepper Roulade

Ingredients – Serves 2

1 bag of fresh spinach, washed and drained

$^1/_2$ tsp nutmeg

$^1/_2$ tsp butter

3tbsp grated parmesan

3tbsp double cream

2 medium eggs, separated

1 large red pepper

200g soft cheese with garlic and herbs

salt and pepper

Method

1. Preheat oven to 190ºC/375ºF/gas mark 5. Line, then grease a Swiss roll tin.
2. Cook the spinach with a tiny amount of water. Drain well by pressing it through a sieve with a spoon. Chop finely and mix with nutmeg, butter, cheese, cream and seasoning.
3. Cool for 5 minutes then beat in egg yolks. Whisk egg whites until they form peaks and fold gently into spinach mixture.
4. Spread into prepared tin. Level and bake for 12-15 minutes until firm.
5. Cook pepper in water then puree or chop finely. Add to cream cheese.
6. Turn spinach mix onto a clean tea towel and leave to cool for half an hour. When cooled peel off the paper. Trim any hard edges, spread with the red pepper cream and carefully roll up using the tea towel. Leave to firm up for 10 minutes then cut into thick slices.
7. Can be served cold. If served hot then add more parmesan and heat for a further 15 minutes.

There's something cooking...

Pat Harrison, Leicester

Luxury Cauliflower Cheese

Ingredients – Serves 4

1 cauliflower cut into florettes

4 slices of cooked bacon cut into pieces

2 hard boiled eggs

2 tomatoes, sliced

for the cheese sauce:

1 tbsp cornflour

300ml milk

12.5g butter

120g cheese (add extra for a cheesier sauce)

salt and pepper

Method

1. Steam the cauliflower, drain and put into an ovenproof dish.
2. Add the bacon.
3. Chop the eggs into 8 pieces and add to the bacon and cauliflower.
4. For the sauce, add all the sauce ingredients to a small pan. Stir until thick. Add to cauliflower mixture and decorate with tomato slices.
5. Cook in a pre-heated oven at 200°C/400°F/gas mark 6 for 20 minutes until golden.

Cheesy Marrow

Ingredients – Serves 4

1 medium marrow

75g butter

1 onion, grated

1 clove of garlic

1 red or green pepper, chopped

200g tomatoes, chopped

100g of crumbly cheese (Lancashire or Wensleydale)

Method

1. Peel the marrow, cut into 2.5cm cubes and remove the seeds.
2. Melt half the butter and fry the marrow until golden brown (approximately 6 minutes).
3. Drain and transfer to a 20cm oven dish .
4. Add the onion, garlic and pepper into a pan with the remaining butter. Add the marrow and tomatoes and mix well.
5. Put half the mixture in an ovenproof dish and add half the cheese. Add the remainder of the marrow mixture and cover with the rest of the cheese.
6. Bake uncovered in the oven at 190ºC/375ºF/gas mark 5 for 30 minutes. Serve with crusty bread or cold with salad.

Emily Cocker, Sheffield

Butter Bean, Olive and Feta Salad

Ingredients – Serves 4

4 tomatoes

4tbsp olive oil

juice of 1 lemon

800g tinned butter beans, drained

50g pitted black olives

1 small red onion, thinly sliced

200g feta cheese, crumbled

handful of fresh parsley, chopped

pitta bread

salt and pepper

Method

1. Chop one of the tomatoes and put it in the food processor or blender with the olive oil and lemon juice. Whizz until fairly smooth.
2. Cut the remaining tomatoes into wedges and mix with the beans, olives, onion, feta and parsley. Season with salt and pepper.
3. Toss in the tomato dressing and serve with pitta bread.

Helen Blackburn, Kettering

There's something cooking...

Beany Burgers with Corn and Apple Relish

Ingredients – Serves 6

for the Beany Burgers:

1 small carrot, grated

1 onion, diced

1 stick of celery, chopped

1 clove of garlic, crushed

75ml olive oil

400g black beans, pinto beans, red kidney beans or green/brown lentils

100g cooked brown rice

handful of parsley

1 vegetable stock cube or 5ml spoon bouillon powder

75g fresh wholewheat breadcrumbs, sesame seeds or oat flakes to coat

salt and pepper

for the Corn and Apple Relish:

2 salad onions, finely chopped

1 green apple, diced

½ red pepper, diced

½ green pepper, diced

small can of sweetcorn, drained

15ml rice or white wine vinegar

fresh parsley, chopped

15ml lemon juice

salt and pepper

Method

1. Sauté the carrot, onion, celery and garlic in 30ml of olive oil for approximately 5 minutes until soft.
2. Drain and add the beans and cooked rice to the pan.
3. Add the parsley, bouillon powder or stock cube, salt and pepper. Mix well and mash everything together.
4. Cool before shaping the mixture into burgers, about 10cm in diameter and 2.5cm thick.
5. Coat with wholewheat breadcrumbs, sesame seeds or oat flakes.
6. Shallow fry in 45ml of olive oil over a medium heat for approximately 3-4 minutes on each side.
7. Serve in a sesame bun with a crisp, green salad and a portion of Corn and Apple Relish which is made by combining all ingredients in a bowl and refrigerating for 30 minutes before serving.

Chicken and Mango Mayonnaise

Ingredients – Serves 4

bouquet garni

1 pint of water

1 tsp vinegar

4 chicken breast fillets

1 large tin of mango slices

150ml mayonnaise

150ml natural yoghurt

chives to taste

1 clove of garlic, crushed

cayenne pepper to taste

salt and ground black pepper to taste

Method

1. Add bouquet garni to the water and bring to the boil. Add vinegar and chicken. Simmer gently for 30 minutes or until chicken is cooked.
2. Remove chicken, cool and chop into bite size pieces.
3. Drain mangos and mash until smooth. Add mayonnaise, yoghurt, chopped chives and garlic.
4. Season to taste with salt, pepper and cayenne pepper.
5. Add chicken and stir.
6. Serve with salad and cous cous.

Delicious Dishes...

Something more substantial

Carlo Cavaliere, Chief Executive,
Congregational & General Insurance

Ragu Cavaliere

Ingredients – Serves 4

extra virgin olive oil

5 garlic cloves, crushed

1 small onion, finely chopped

4 Italian pork sausage (or similar) with links and casing removed, finely chopped

large glass of good quality red wine, for example Chianti Classico, Brunello or another Tuscan wine

4 chopped Italian tomatoes

fresh parsley and basil, chopped

salt and black pepper

1 small red chilli or ground flakes

400g dried or fresh pasta, for example Pici or Lumaconi

parmesan cheese, grated

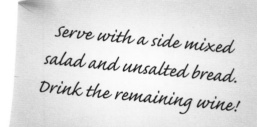

Serve with a side mixed salad and unsalted bread. Drink the remaining wine!

Method

1. Heat the olive oil in a suitable pan and add the garlic and onion.
2. Cook until the onions soften and colour.
3. Add the minced sausage meat and cook until coloured.
4. Add the wine and cook until it has almost been absorbed.
5. Add the tomatoes, parsley, basil, salt, pepper and chilli and stir well.
6. Simmer and cook for approximately 1 hour, with regular stirring.
7. Cook the pasta in boiling water, with a little olive oil (do not add salt) until it is *al dente* and drain.
8. Return the pasta to the pan, adding some sauce and stir in.
9. Serve in individual pasta bowls with additional sauce and Parmesan cheese.

Brian's Spanish-Style Fish Stew

Ingredients – Serves 4-6

3tbsp olive oil

2 large onions

4 cloves of garlic

approximately 250ml dry white wine

a few strands of saffron

1kg fresh tomatoes or two cans of chopped tomatoes

1 green pepper

a sprinkle of chilli flakes, to taste

2tsp of fennel seeds

250ml fish or veg stock

1 whole red snapper about 500g, cut into four large pieces. (Alternatively, use 2-4 small red mullet)

1 whole sea bream or bass, cleaned and scaled, cut into four large slices

2 fillets of white fish such as hake or haddock, about 200g each, cut into chunks

approximately 12 medium-sized raw king prawns

approximately 20 fresh mussels, in shells, cleaned with beards removed (optional)

2tbsp chopped parsley

salt and pepper

Method

1. Begin by heating the olive oil in a large saucepan or wok. Gently fry the onions and garlic until soft but not brown. In another small pan, warm the white wine and add the saffron.

2. While the onions and garlic are cooking, skin, de-seed and chop the fresh tomatoes. De-seed the pepper and chop it into strips.

3. Add the tomatoes, pepper, chilli flakes and fennel seeds to the softened onions and garlic. Stir and add the white wine and saffron, then about half of the stock. Season with salt and pepper.

4. Leave the pan uncovered, simmering gently while the liquid reduces to about half its volume. This could take 30-40 minutes. Use the rest of the stock to thin out the stew if it becomes too thick. Ideally, it should have the consistency of a thick soup.

5. About 25 minutes from serving time, add the fish, except the prawns and mussels, continue to simmer gently. Taste and adjust the seasoning.

6. With around 10 minutes to go you should add the king prawns, mussels and parsley. Serve with crusty bread.

Bring to the table piping hot, in the cooking vessel, and serve with lots of fresh crusty bread.

A Congregational Casserole

Ingredients – Serves 6-8

400g pork, chopped

1 onion, chopped

400g leeks, chopped

1tsp olive oil

400g swede, diced

2 large carrots, sliced

½ pint chicken stock

50g baked beans

1tbsp mixed herbs

Method

1. Sauté the diced pork, onions and leeks in the olive oil.
2. Add swede, carrots and stock to pork mixture.
3. Bring to the boil and simmer until the vegetables are cooked but firm, adding water as necessary.
4. Add the baked beans and mixed herbs.
5. Turn into a casserole dish and cook in a pre-heated oven at 180ºC/350ºF/gas mark 4 for 45 minutes.

Wayne Hawkins, President Elect,
Congregational Federation

Chicken stuffed with Black Pudding wrapped in Bacon in a Creamy Peppercorn Sauce

Ingredients – Serves 4

4 chicken breast fillets

200g black pudding

4 rashers of bacon

250ml double cream

1 tbsp cracked peppercorns

1 tsp sherry

salt

Method

1. Butterfly the chicken breasts.
2. Divide the black pudding into 4 and place a piece in each chicken breast. Fold the breast back together.
3. Wrap a rasher of bacon around each of the chicken breasts.
4. Wrap in tin foil and place in a pre-heated oven at 200°C/400°F/gas mark 6 for 20 minutes. Remove the foil and cook for a further 10 minutes until browned.
5. Pour the cream into a pan and add a pinch of salt, peppercorns and sherry.
6. Bring to the boil.
7. Place chicken on a plate and pour the sauce over.
8. Serve immediately with chips or well seasoned mash.

Congregational

Protecting the things you value since 1891

Jonny Procter, Cumbria

There's something cooking...

Salmon with Honey Sauce

Ingredients – Serves 4

juice and zest of one lime

1 tbsp wholegrain mustard

3 tbsp clear honey

clove of garlic, crushed

4 salmon steaks

Reverend Jonathan Edwards,
General Secretary, Baptist Union of Great Britain

Method

1. Mix together the juice and zest of the lime, wholegrain mustard, honey and the crushed clove of garlic.
2. Spread the marinade over the salmon steaks and leave for 5-10 minutes.
3. Cook the steaks at 200°C/400°F/gas mark 6 for approximately 7-8 minutes until golden on top and cooked in the middle.

Congregational

Protecting the things you value since 1891

Italian Meatballs

Ingredients

for the meatballs:

400g pork or beef mince

1 clove of garlic, chopped finely

2 slices of bread made into crumbs

½ tsp dried oregano

1 medium egg, beaten

grated parmesan cheese

oil

flour

salt and pepper

for the tomato sauce:

1 tin of tomatoes

1 onion, chopped

1 garlic clove, crushed

olive oil

½ tsp dried oregano

1 tbsp tomato puree

water

Method

For the meatballs:

1. Add all the meatball ingredients together except for the cheese, flour and oil in a bowl and mix.
2. Shape the mixture into balls about the size of a golf ball.
3. Roll the meatballs in the flour and fry gently in the oil, turning occasionally until lightly browned.

For the tomato sauce:

1. Fry the onion very gently in the oil until soft and add the crushed garlic and oregano. Fry for 1 minute then add the tomatoes and puree. Fill the empty tin full of water and add along with the salt and pepper.
2. Gently cook for 10 minutes. Add the meatballs and cook slowly for 1 hour. If the sauce looks too thick add more water.
3. Serve with spaghetti and grated parmesan cheese on top.

Mrs Janet Wood, Bradford

Spicy Fish Pie

Ingredients – Serves 4

1 pint milk	75g butter
2 bay leaves	50g plain flour
10 peppercorns	1 tbsp curry paste
1 onion	2tbsp coriander, chopped
175g salmon fillet	zest and juice from 1 lime
175g cod fillet	400g potatoes
175g prawns	2tbsp milk for mash
175g haddock fillet	salt and pepper

Method

1. Put milk, bay leaves, peppercorns and chopped onion into a pan. Add all the fish and bring to boil. Cook for 2 minutes.
2. Strain all fish from pan and remove any skin and bones.
3. Flake the fish into a baking dish, ensuring there is an even distribution of different fish across the dish.
4. Strain milk into a pan and discard remaining ingredients.
5. Melt 50g of butter in pan and stir in flour and curry paste. Stir together for 1 minute. Remove from heat and gradually stir in the reserved milk.
6. Bring to boil and cook until thickened for approximately 4 minutes. Add chopped coriander, lime zest and juice. Pour sauce over the fish.
7. For the topping boil the potatoes. Once cooked, mash adding 25g of butter and 2tbsp of milk. Season with salt and ground pepper to taste.
8. Place mashed potatoes over fish mixture using fork to create even distribution across the top. Cook in a pre-heated oven for 30 minutes at 200°C/400°F/gas mark 6.

Margaret Slater, Ilkley

Spaghetti alle Vongole

This also makes a nice seafood pasta by substituting the clams with mixed seafood.

Ingredients – Serves 2

olive oil

4 cloves of garlic, chopped or crushed

1 tin of chopped tomatoes

1 tin of baby clams, drained and liquid reserved

200g dried spaghetti

large handful of fresh flatleaf parsley, chopped

splash of fish sauce (optional)

grated parmesan

12 cherry tomatoes (optional)

salt and pepper

Method

1. Warm the olive oil in a frying pan or large saucepan and sweat the garlic gently.
2. Add the tomatoes and clam liquid and simmer for ten minutes.
3. Bring a large pan of water to the boil and cook the spaghetti.
4. 5 minutes before the spaghetti is cooked add the parsley, clams and fish sauce if required to the tomato sauce.
5. Continue to simmer until the spaghetti is cooked.
6. Drain the spaghetti and add it to the sauce to coat. Serve with halved cherry tomatoes and grated parmesan to taste.

Congregational
Protecting the things you value since 1891

There's something cooking...

Katie Wood, York

Game Pie

an use pigeon, partridge or pretty much any other game meat. If using a small bird like woodcock pluck and draw but leave whole.

Ingredients – Serves 6-8

40g butter

4 pheasant breasts, diced

2 duck breasts, diced

350g bacon rashers, rinded and diced

2 large onions, sliced

3 large carrots, sliced

4 celery sticks, sliced

600ml beef stock

225ml red wine

1 bay leaf

1 tbsp cornflour

2 tbsp port or sherry

3 tbsp redcurrant jelly

225g puff pastry

egg, beaten to glaze

salt and fresh ground black pepper

Method

1. Melt the butter in a large pan, add the pheasant and duck and fry over a moderate heat until browned, then remove from pan. Add the bacon and onions and brown lightly.

2. Return pheasant and duck pieces to the pan with the carrots, celery, stock and wine. Bring to the boil, season well and add the bay leaf. Cover and simmer for 1-1 hour 30 minutes until tender.

3. Strain off the juices into a small pan. Cool the meat slightly (at this point if you are using a woodcock remove the flesh from the bones) and place in a pie dish with the bacon and vegetables.

4. Blend the cornflour with the port, add some of the hot juices and mix. Add back to main pan with redcurrant jelly. Bring to boil, stirring until slightly reduced. Pour into the pie dish.

5. Roll out pastry slightly larger than the top of the pie dish. Cut off a strip 2.5cm wide and fit onto the dampened rim of the pie dish. Brush the pastry rim with beaten egg and add the pastry lid. Press the edges firmly together, then trim and flute.

6. You can make use of any trimmings to make leaves to decorate the lid. Brush the lid with beaten egg and make a hole in the centre adding your leaves.

7. Bake the pie in a pre-heated oven at 220°C/425°F/gas mark 7 for 20 minutes reducing the temperature to 190°C/375°F/gas mark 5 and bake for a further 20-30 minutes until well browned.

8. Serve with mash and vegetables.

Robert Procter, Cumbria

Scouse

Ingredients – Serves 8

750g stewing steak

180g neck end of lamb

1 lamb leg bone (pre-cooked)

1kg King Edward potatoes

450g root vegetables

1 large onion

handful of pot herbs

salt and pepper

Method

1. Cover the meat and bones with water and simmer for approximately 45 minutes. While it is cooking prepare the vegetables by cutting them into chunks.
2. Add the vegetables to the pan and bring to the boil. Turn the heat down and allow to simmer for as long as it takes to ensure the meat is tender. When necessary add water to keep contents covered.
3. Season to taste, sprinkle with herbs and serve with pickled red cabbage, beetroot or piccalilli.

There's something cooking...

Sheila Fellows, Liverpool

Magret de canard a l`Armagnac

Ingredients – Serves 2

2 duck breasts, de-boned

2dsp Armagnac

75g unsalted butter

3dsp double cream

Method

1. On a very low heat, in a clean, dry sauté pan, sweat the breasts, skin-side down, for 10 minutes. Turn them over for another 10 minutes then flip them over once more, until the outside is brown, and the inside pink.

2. Pour the Armagnac on to the duck and shake the pan. Remove the duck breasts and put them into a heatproof dish, keeping them warm while they rest.

3. Turn back to the pan again and add the butter, little by little, to what is left of the Armagnac, scraping the sides of the pan to collect all the juices. Sizzle until all the brown from the pan is incorporated, and then stir in the cream.

4. Collect any remaining juices from the duck breasts, and pour them into the sauté pan. Slice the duck breasts in two and drizzle over the juices from the sauté pan and serve with seasonal vegetables of your choice.

Deanna Baynes, Cahors, France (Cookery writer for The Church Times)

There's something cooking...

Risotto Con Porcini

Ingredients – Serves 4

750ml vegetable stock

150-170g fresh porcini or ceps or fresh button mushrooms

1 small onion, chopped

cooking oil

15g butter

15g dried porcini, soaked for 15 minutes

170g Arborio rice

knob of butter

30g grated parmesan cheese

salt and pepper

Method

1. Gently heat the pan of stock on the cooker, next to the ring you will use for the rice.
2. Clean the mushrooms carefully and slice. Fry the onion in the oil and butter until it begins to colour. Add the fresh mushrooms, chop the pre-soaked dried mushrooms and add to the pan. Strain the soaking water into the stock.
3. Add the rice to the frying pan and stir until well coated with the butter and oil. Ladle some of the warmed stock into the pan, only as much as is needed to cover, continue to stir and add stock until cooked (approximately 20-25 minutes). Remove the pan from the heat to allow the rice to absorb the rest of the liquid. Do not add more liquid. The risotto should be creamy but the grain still have some 'bite'.
4. Stir in the butter and parmesan before serving. Check seasoning and serve.

There's something cooking...

Peter O'Rourke, Lancaster

Beef Stroganoff

Ingredients – Serves 2-4

1 onion, chopped

oil

400g frying steak, chopped into bite-size strips

250g exotic mushrooms

1 tbsp brandy

2 tsp mustard

2 tbsp crème fraîche

salt and pepper

Method

1. Fry the onion in oil until soft. Add steak and cook for 1 minute. Add mushrooms and cook for a further minute.
2. Add brandy and mustard and stir.
3. Add crème fraîche and stir. Add salt and plenty of black pepper and simmer for 5 minutes.
4. Serve on a bed of rice.

Congregational
Protecting the things you value since 1891

There's something cooking...

Rob Harding, Keighley

Creamy Chicken and Tomato Curry

Ingredients – Serves 4

1 onion, chopped

2tbsp vegetable oil

4 chicken breasts, chopped into bite-size pieces

2 garlic cloves, chopped

2.5cm fresh ginger, finely chopped

1tsp chilli powder

2tsp ground coriander

400g tinned chopped tomatoes

4tbsp crème fraîche

1tbsp plain flour

50ml water

3tbsp fresh coriander, chopped

salt and pepper

Method

1. Fry the onion in vegetable oil for 2-3 minutes. Add chicken and fry until cooked.
2. Add garlic, ginger, chilli, ground coriander and cook for another minute.
3. Add chopped tomatoes and crème fraîche and season with salt and pepper.
4. Mix the flour and water together and add to the pan off the heat. Return to the heat and simmer for 15 minutes.
5. Add fresh coriander and serve immediately with basmati or pilau rice.

Congregational

Protecting the things you value since 1891

Samantha Claxton, Newcastle

There's something cooking...

Leek, Bacon and Root Mash Pie

Ingredients – Serves 4

450g leeks

450g parsnips

450g carrots

$1/2$ small swede

25g butter

300g bacon

300ml milk

1 tsp English mustard

100g grated cheese

2 tbsp cornflour to thicken sauce

black pepper to taste

Method

1. Wash and cut leeks into 2.5cm rings. Steam until cooked and put to one side.
2. Cook parsnips, carrots and swede until tender. Mash with butter and season to taste with black pepper.
3. Chop the bacon into small pieces and cook until crispy. Put to one side.
4. Make a cheese sauce with the milk, butter, mustard, cheese and cornflour.
5. Mix the cheese sauce, bacon and leeks together. Put into a large casserole dish and top with the root mash. Add grated cheese to top.
6. Cook at 200°C/400°F/gas mark 6 for 20 minutes until the cheese has browned. Serve with other vegetables.

Roasted Red Mullet with Spaghetti

Ingredients - Serves 2

100g black olives, pitted

2 dried chillies

200g cherry vine tomatoes

extra-virgin olive oil

2 red mullet fillets

1 tbsp thyme leaves

320g spaghetti or a pasta of your choice

Method

1. Pre-heat the oven to 200°C/400°F/gas mark 6. Stone the olives if required and crumble the chillies.
2. Toss the tomatoes in a little olive oil. Season and place in a baking tin. Prick each with a fork. Roast in the oven for 20 minutes.
3. Place the mullet fillets in one layer in a shallow baking dish, and sprinkle with thyme and chilli. Season. Drizzle with olive oil and roast in the oven for 5 minutes.
4. Cook the pasta in boiling salted water for 10 minutes or until *al dente*. Drain and return to the pan.
5. Add the olives and tomatoes to the pasta with a tablespoon of olive oil, and season. Add the mullet and toss gently. Serve at once.

Sally Hetherington, Berkshire

There's something cooking...

Steak and Kidney Stew with Herb Dumplings

Ingredients – Serves 4-6

for the stew:

olive oil

1 onion, sliced

cubetti de panacetta or bacon

1 slice black pudding, finely chopped

5 reasonable sized lambs kidneys, cored and diced

600g sirloin steak, trimmed and diced

plain white flour, seasoned

1 tsp coriander

1 tsp cumin powder

½ bottle of red wine, Shiraz or something similar

1kg vegetable stew pack or fresh root vegetables such as carrot, swede, potato, parsnip and celery

¾ tsp redcurrant jelly

¾ tsp Bovril

Worcester sauce

4-8 garlic cloves, peeled

3 bay leafs

handful of dried mixed herbs

tomato purée

5 open cup mushrooms

beef stock cube

1.5 tsp salt

½ tsp pepper

for the dumplings:

100g white self-raising flour

50g suet

dried mixed herbs

pinch of salt

Method

1. Heat some olive oil in a large frying pan and add the onion and half a teaspoon of salt to prevent the onion caramelising. Once softened, add the cubetti de panacetta or bacon and black pudding.

2. Coat the kidney and steak with the seasoned flour. Add to the pan to brown. As the meat pieces brown, remove from the pan and place in a large casserole dish.

3. What appears to be burnt flour will appear on the bottom of the pan. You might need to add some more oil to the pan.

4. Add the coriander, cumin and pepper. Fry these for approximately one minute, and then add half a bottle of red wine. Deglaze the pan with the wine, and boil gently until the alcohol is removed.

5. Add the veg. Keep on the heat, and when the veg has started to cook add the redcurrant jelly, Bovril, a splash of Worcester sauce, garlic cloves, bay leafs, dried mixed herbs, a teaspoon of salt, a squirt of tomato puree, mushrooms and the beef stock cube (sprinkled over the mix).

6. Stir this together and decide whether or not you think it needs more liquid. If so, add some hot water. When this is mixed up, transfer from the pan into the casserole dish and stir once more to distribute the meat throughout the mix.

7. Put a lid on the casserole and place in a pre-heated oven at 180°C/350°F/gas mark 4. The stew will take 2-3 hours to cook. How long it takes depends on the quality of steak used. If you use shin beef you will need 3 hours but if you use fillet or sirloin then 2 hours will be enough. Check on the stew a couple of times and stir, adding a bit more hot water if you think it is getting too thick.

8. About 25 minutes before the end of cooking time, start to make the dumplings. You need a ratio of 2:1 flour to suet. Mix the suet and flour with a fork dry to start with. Add a pinch of salt and the dried mixed herbs, then add a little water to the mix and stir. You are aiming for a consistency of bread dough, so add a little water at a time.

9. Take the stew out of the oven, and divide the dumpling mix into 4-6 balls and place on the top of the stew.

10. Replace the lid on the casserole dish and return to the oven. Turn the oven up to 190°C/375°F/gas mark 5.

11. Check the stew and dumplings after 20 minutes. The dumplings should be cooked through and not sticky in the middle.

There's something cooking...

Martin Scott, Technical Director, Congregational & General Insurance

Cod with Tomato and White Wine Sauce

Ingredients – Serves 4

1 medium sized onion

1 clove of garlic

1 dsp vegetable oil

25g plain flour

4 tbsp dry white wine

350g chopped tomatoes

20 black olives, pitted

4 cod steaks or tail end pieces of cod (allow 150g per person)

bunch fresh parsley

salt and pepper

Alternative sustainable fish varieties can be used such as lemon sole, talapia or red snapper

Method

1. Slice onion and crush the garlic into a paste.
2. Heat the oil in a pan and add the onion and garlic. Fry until soft but with no colour.
3. Stir flour into the pan and cook for 1 minute without browning the flour
4. Add the wine, tomatoes and pitted black olives, stirring all the time. Bring to the boil and simmer for 1 minute.
5. Transfer mixture to an ovenproof dish.
6. Arrange the fish on top of the sauce mixture and cover the dish with foil. Bake for 25-30 minutes, garnish with sprigs of parsley.
7. Serve with boiled whole potatoes or jacket potatoes and garden peas or asparagus.

Congregational

Protecting the things you value since 1891

Peter Wakefield, Calverton, Nottingham

Herby Sausage Jambalaya

Ingredients – Serves 4

450g small Lincolnshire sausages

1 tsp oil

1 onion, chopped

2 cloves of garlic, crushed

1 tsp chilli powder

2 tsp ground turmeric

225g brown rice

450ml stock

400g chopped tomatoes

5 spring onions, chopped

1 courgette, sliced

½ red pepper, seeded and chopped

100g button mushroom, quartered

100g cooked and peeled prawns (optional)

salt and black pepper

Method

1. Halve each sausage. Heat the oil in a large saucepan and cook the sausages over a medium heat until browned.
2. Add the onion, garlic, chilli powder, turmeric and rice and cook until rice is opaque. Add stock, chopped tomatoes and seasoning.
3. Bring to the boil, cover and simmer for 20 minutes. Add the remaining ingredients and continue to cook, uncovered, for a further 10 minutes or until liquid is absorbed.
4. Serve with a mixed salad.

Luxury Cottage Pie

Ingredients – Serves 6

2tsp sunflower oil

2 leeks, sliced and washed

150g carrots, diced

2 cloves of garlic, crushed

675g lean minced beef

900ml beef stock

20ml Worcestershire sauce

4tbsp tomato puree

100g button mushrooms, wiped, trimmed and sliced

30ml fresh, chopped parsley

40g margarine or butter

40g plain flour

450ml milk

pinch of dry mustard

50g cheddar cheese, grated

675g potatoes, boiled until tender

675g parsnips, boiled until tender

2 large eggs, separated

salt and pepper

Method

1. Heat the oil in a large pan. Fry the leeks, carrots and garlic for about 2 minutes to soften slightly, then add the minced beef. Stir to break up any large chunks of meat and fry for about 5 minutes, turning until browned all over.

2. Stir in the beef stock, Worcestershire sauce and tomato puree. Bring to the boil, reduce heat and simmer for 25 minutes. Add mushrooms and chopped parsley, season to taste and cook for a further 5 minutes. Spoon into a large ovenproof dish.

3. Melt the butter in a pan, stir in the flour and cook for 1 minute. Gradually add the milk to form a smooth sauce. Season, then add mustard and cheese. Mash warm boiled potatoes and parsnips together, stir in cheese sauce and egg yolks.

4. Whisk egg whites until stiff, then gently fold in potato and parsnip mixture. Lightly spoon potato topping over mince, fork up the surface and bake at 200°C/400°F/gas mark 6 for 25 minutes until golden.

Congregational
Protecting the things you value since 1891

Pesto Cod

Alternative sustainable varieties can be used such as pollock or coley

Ingredients – Serves 2

for the pesto:

100ml olive oil

1 bunch of fresh basil

2 cloves of garlic

100g pine nuts

for the cod:

150g potatoes

2 cod fillets, de-boned

2 medium tomatoes, skinned and deseeded

Method

1. In a blender, make the pesto by whizzing together the olive oil, basil, garlic and pine nuts.
2. Cook the potatoes, mash and add the pesto. Place the mixture on top of the cod on a lined baking tray.
3. Put the sliced tomatoes on top.
4. Place in a pre-heated oven at 200°C/400°F/gas mark 6 for approximately 10-15 minutes until the cod is cooked, garnish with basil and serve with a salad.

There's something cooking...

Nicola Parker, Surrey

Sizzling Sausage Casserole

Serve with plenty of creamy mashed potatoes

Ingredients - Serves 4

12 good pork sausages

1 large onion

2 cloves of garlic, chopped

1 420g can of baked beans

1 420g can of chopped tomatoes

mixed dried herbs

salt and pepper

Method

1. Lightly brown the sausages in a pan.
2. In the meantime put the chopped onion, garlic, baked beans and chopped tomatoes into a casserole dish.
3. Add to the sauce along with the salt, pepper and herbs.
4. Cover the dish and place in a pre-heated oven at 220°C/425°F/gas mark 7 for one hour.

Katie Smith, South Wirral

There's something cooking...

Divine Desserts

...and sweet delights

Apple Meringue Pie

Method

1. Break up the trifle sponges and put in an oven proof dish.

2. Peel, core and cook the apples in a pan with the granulated sugar. Add them to the trifle sponges.

3. Separate the eggs and whisk the egg whites with the caster sugar until it peaks.

4. Add egg white to the top of the trifle sponges and apples.

5. Bake in the oven at 200ºC/400ºF/gas mark 6 for 20 minutes or until golden. Serve hot or cold with cream.

Ingredients – Serves 4-6

160g packet of trifle sponges

450g cooking apples

50g granulated sugar

3 medium egg whites

100g caster sugar

Agnes May Brannan, Edinburgh

There's something cooking...

Apple Crumble

Ingredients – Serves 4-6

100g sugar

200g self raising flour

100g butter

7 medium apples, cooking or eating

cinnamon stick

Method

1. Mix in the sugar and flour together in a dish

2. Add the butter to the dry ingredients and crumble the mixture between your fingers until you have desired texture.

3. Skin and cut apples into chunks or slices. Add two tablespoons of water to a pan and a dessertspoon of sugar. Add apples and cinnamon stick. Stew for 5 minutes on a low heat.

4. Remove the cinnamon stick and put the softened apples into a baking dish. Cover apples with crumble mixture (lightly sprinkle, don't pat down).

5. Put in the oven at 190°C/375°F/gas mark 5 for 20-30 minutes, until golden.

Five Minute Chocolate Mug Cake

Ingredients – Serves 1

4tbsp flour

4tbsp sugar

2tbsp cocoa

1 medium egg

3tbsp milk

3tbsp oil

3tbsp chocolate chips (optional)

small splash vanilla extract

1 large coffee mug

Method

1. Add the dry ingredients to the mug and mix well. Add the egg and mix thoroughly. Pour in the milk and oil and mix well. Add the chocolate chips (if using) and vanilla extract and mix again.

2. Put your mug in the microwave and cook for 3 minutes at 1000 watts (high). The cake will rise to the top of the mug. Allow to cool a little and tip out on a plate if desired.

Ann Scott, Baildon, West Yorkshire

Easy Lemon Mousse

Ingredients – Serves 1

2 large eggs

100g sugar

4 lemons

12g gelatine

3tbsp cold water

Method

1. Separate the eggs. Place the yolk and sugar in a bowl and beat until creamy.

2. Grate the lemon rind and squeeze the juice. Add to the mixture.

3. Put the gelatine in a cup with the water and leave to stand for 3 minutes until spongy. Place in a microwave on full power for 1 minute to dissolve, then cool slightly and stir into the lemon mixture.

4. Whisk the egg whites.

5. Fold into the lemon mixture.

6. Leave to set in the fridge for 30 minutes.

Rita Goodson, Manchester

If desired you could add mixed spice, cinnamon or nutmeg. Orange or lemon zest gives it a tang.

Bread and Butter Pudding

Ingredients – Serves 6

2 medium eggs

25g sugar

400ml milk

6 slices bread and butter

50g currants or mixed dried fruit

Method

1. Beat the eggs, sugar and milk together to make the custard. It can then be heated on the hob or in the microwave.
2. Cut the buttered bread into small squares and layer into an ovenproof dish. Sprinkle with layers of dried fruit.
3. Pour the custard over and let it soak for approximately half an hour.
4. Bake in a moderate oven at 180°C/350°F/gas mark 4 until the pudding is set, risen and golden.

Commissioner John Matear, Territorial Commander, Salvation Army

There's something cooking...

Taste of Heaven

Ingredients

strawberries, approximately 3 large ones per bagel

cinnamon and raisin bagel

cream cheese or clotted cream

dark chocolate, about 2 squares

Method

1. Slice the strawberries into horizontal slices.
2. Toast the bagel.
3. Smear with clotted cream or cream cheese.
4. Arrange strawberries in a flower shape on top of the cream.
5. Grate dark chocolate finely and sprinkle on top.

Congregational

Protecting the things you value since 1891

Margaret Hitchman, Bournemouth

Citrus Fruit Tart

Ingredients – Serves 6-8

4 large eggs, yolks only

400g can of sweetened, condensed milk

zest and juice of 1 lemon

zest and juice of 1 lime

3 small oranges

1 ready-made sweet pastry case

3tbsp apricot jam

Method

1. Pre-heat the oven to 160°C/325°F/gas mark 3. Whisk together the egg yolks, condensed milk, lemon, lime and one orange zest and juice until smooth.

2. Pour the mixture into the cooked pastry case and bake for 30-35 minutes until firm to the touch. Leave to cool. Remove the skin from the remaining two oranges and cut into slices, then cut each slice in half. Arrange the orange halves around the edge of the tart so they are slightly overlapping.

3. Warm the apricot jam, push through a fine sieve then add 1 tablespoon of water. Pour a little over the centre of the tart so that it is evenly covered, then brush the orange slices with the remaining jam. Chill for approximately 1 hour before serving.

4. Garnish with thin strips of orange zest.

Congregational

Protecting the things you value since 1891

John Hakes, Plymouth

Teatime Treats...

Put the kettle on and relax

Beautiful Banana and Carrot Muffins

Ingredients

1 large egg, beaten

60ml melted butter or margarine

1 medium carrot, grated

1 banana, mashed

60g soft brown sugar

30ml sultanas, blueberries, cranberries, chopped dried apricots or dates

125ml milk

150g self raising flour

5ml baking powder

pinch of mixed spice or cinnamon

optional chopped nuts for topping

Method

1. Preheat the oven to 200°C/400°F/gas mark 6.
2. Prepare muffin tins - either grease or line with muffin cases.
3. Combine the egg, melted butter/margarine, grated carrot, mashed banana, sugar, dried fruit and milk in a large mixing bowl.
4. In a smaller bowl sieve together the flour, baking powder and mixed spice.
5. Combine both mixtures in the large mixing bowl and fold together until just mixed (do not beat as this will result in tough muffins).
6. Spoon the batter into the greased muffin tins or muffin cases filling them about three quarters full.
7. Bake for 20-30 minutes until golden brown, light and fluffy.
8. Allow muffins to cool before turning out onto a cooling rack.

Fluffy Cloud Lemon Cake

Ingredients

30g butter

8 large eggs, separated

pinch of salt

250g caster sugar

100g plain flour

zest of two lemons, finely grated

icing sugar

Method

1. Pre-heat the oven to 180°C/350°F/gas mark 4 and grease a 20cm cake tin with the butter.

2. Pour the egg whites into a mixing bowl, with the salt and beat them until they stand in soft peaks.

3. Whisk the sugar in to make a meringue mixture. Whisk the egg yolks in another bowl then carefully add to the meringue mixture.

4. Fold in the flour and lemon zest and whisk for a further 15 seconds.

5. Spoon the mixture into the prepared cake tin and cook for approximately 45 minutes. Cover with foil if starting to brown too quickly.

6. Turn the cake onto a rack to cool. It will naturally sink in the middle. Dust with icing sugar to finish.

Sophie Spyropoulos, Harrogate

There's something cooking...

Great fun can be had by making the biscuits into Gingerbread Men and decorating for Christmas!

The Most Reverend and Right Honourable the Lord Archbishop of Canterbury, Rowan Williams, Church of England

Ginger Biscuits

Ingredients

100g margarine

150g granulated sugar

1 medium egg

75g golden syrup, warmed

300g self raising flour

2tsp ground ginger

1tsp bicarbonate of soda

Method

1. Cream the margarine and sugar together until well blended.

2. Beat in the egg and the warm golden syrup.

3. Stir the dry ingredients together and add gradually to the mixture.

4. Roll into walnut sized balls and bake on a greased baking tray at 150ºC/300ºF/gas mark 2 for 10-15 minutes. Alternatively use a cutter to form gingerbread men.

5. Leave to cool on the tray.

Congregational

Protecting the things you value since 1891

There's something cooking...

Altar Ego Victoria Sponge

Ingredients

125g self raising flour

1 level tsp baking powder

pinch of salt

115g caster sugar

7tbsp cooking oil

2 large eggs

2tbsp milk

few drops of vanilla essence

jam

cream or buttercream

Method

1. Grease a 5 x 17.5cm sandwich cake tin and line the base with greaseproof paper.
2. Sift flour, baking powder and salt into a bowl and stir in the sugar.
3. Add oil, eggs, milk and essence.
4. Mix until blended and creamy for approximately 2 minutes.
5. Put into a well-greased baking tin and bake in the centre of the oven for 35-40 minutes at 180ºC/350ºF/gas mark 4.
6. Remove from tin and when cool cut open, then sandwich together with jam and cream.

Congregational

Protecting the things you value since 1891

Simone Price, Cirencester

Cherry Scones

Ingredients

50g butter

225g self raising flour

25g caster sugar

50g glace cherries, roughly chopped

25g crunchy wheatgerm (optional)

$^1/_4$ pint milk

Method

1. In a bowl rub the butter into the flour until you get something that looks like breadcrumbs and stir in the caster sugar.

2. Stir the cherries into the flour mixture until evenly distributed then add the wheatgerm.

3. Mix to a soft dough slowly adding the milk, kneading lightly until you get a smooth consistency.

4. Roll out the dough to approx 2cm. Use a circular cutter to cut out scone shapes.

5. Place the scones on a preheated baking sheet, brush top with milk and bake at 230°C/400°F/gas mark 8 for 10-12 minutes. Leave to cool.

6. Serve immediately, split and spread with butter.

Congregational

Protecting the things you value since 1891

Eloise Garrett, Leeds

There's something cooking...

Breakfast Bars

These bars last well in an airtight tin.

Ingredients

397g can of condensed milk

250g porridge oats

75g desiccated coconut

100g dried berries

125g mixed raw nuts

125g mixed raw seeds

Gillian Ashmore, Recording Clerk, Religious Society of Friends (Quakers)

Method

1. Heat the condensed milk gently until runny.
2. Mix the dry ingredients together and combine with the warm milk.
3. Pour into a well greased baking pan (approximately 30 x 20cm) and smooth down the surface.
4. Bake for approximately 1 hour at 160°C/325°F/gas mark 3.
5. Leave to cool in the pan and mark into squares, so that there is enough for 12 big or 15 medium bars.

Congregational

Protecting the things you value since 1891

Mum's Tablet

Ingredients

900g sugar

100g butter

250ml milk

400g sweetened condensed milk

1tsp vanilla essence

Method

1. Put the sugar, butter and milk in a large pot.

2. Heat gently on a low heat for approximately 45 minutes and stir frequently until the sugar has dissolved.

3. Add the condensed milk and stir continuously until boiling and the mixture attains a rich, creamy, golden colour.

4. Continue stirring as it can burn easily. This will take half an hour.

5. Remove from the heat, add vanilla essence, and beat with an electric whisk until the mixtures thickens, for approximately 5-10 minutes.

6. Pour the mixture into a greased Swiss roll tin 33 x 20cm, mark into squares and leave to cool.

Sheila Redwood, Provincial President of Mothers Union in Scotland, on behalf of the Scottish Episcopal Church

There's something cooking...

Bara Brith

Ingredients

400g mixed fruit

150g brown sugar

½ pint strained warm tea

400g self raising flour

1 tsp mixed spice

2 tbsp warm marmalade

1 medium egg, beaten

Reverend D Haydn Thomas,
Moderator,
Presbyterian Church of Wales

Congregational
Protecting the things you value since 1891

Method

1. Place the fruit and sugar into a mixing bowl and soak overnight in the strained tea.
2. Sieve the flour and mixed spice, and warm the marmalade.
3. Add the flour, mixed spice, warm marmalade and beaten egg to the soaked fruit and mix well.
4. Pour the mixture into a greased loaf tin 23 x 13cm.
5. Bake for approximately 1 hour 20 minutes at 180°C/350°F/gas mark 4.
6. Cool on a wire rack.
7. Serve sliced and buttered.

Choco Chip Cookies

Ingredients

115g butter

110g soft brown sugar

50g caster sugar

1 medium egg, beaten

3 drops of vanilla extract

170g chocolate chips of your choice

155g plain flour

pinch of baking powder

Method

1. Pre-heat the oven to 180°C/350°F/gas mark 4 and line a baking tray with greaseproof paper.
2. Cream the butter and sugars together until light and fluffy. Add the beaten egg and vanilla to the mixture and mix well.
3. Add the chocolate chips and mix together to ensure they are well distributed.
4. Mix the flour and baking powder together, and add a little at a time to the mixture, until a soft dough is formed. You should be able to mould the dough into shapes without it being too sticky. If it is, add a tablespoon of flour at a time to get the desired consistency.
5. Roll into a ball about the size of a walnut and softly press down onto the baking sheet. Don't place cookies too close together as they do spread and you don't want them to stick together.
6. Cook for 10-12 minutes. When you take them out of the oven they will still be quite soft, so leave to cool on the tray before moving them to a cooling rack.

Tamarind Wilson-Flint, Bramhope

Banana Cake

Ingredients

100g margarine

200g plain flour

300g Demerara sugar

2 large eggs

2tbsp milk

2 ripe bananas, mashed

squirt of lemon juice

1tsp bicarbonate of soda

chopped walnuts or pecans, optional

Reverend Dr Martyn Atkins,
General Secretary, Methodist Church

Method

1. Rub together the margarine and plain flour.

2. Add the sugar, eggs and milk and mix together with the mashed bananas, lemon juice, bicarbonate of soda and nuts.

3. Continue mixing until a smooth consistency and put into a greased, lined loaf tin 23 x 13cm.

4. Cook at 170°C/325°F/gas mark 3 for approximately 1 hour.

Congregational

Protecting the things you value since 1891

Ecclefechan Tart

Ingredients

for the pastry:

175g plain flour

75g butter

1 large egg

for the filling:

100g butter

350g sultanas

4 large eggs

100g demerara sugar

2 tbsp white wine vinegar

Method

1. Sift the flour into a bowl, cut the butter into small cubes and rub into the flour until you get breadcrumbs.
2. Add the beaten egg and bring the dough together with a knife.
3. Place the pastry dough on a lightly dusted board and roll out and line a 20cm flan dish then rest for 30 minutes.
4. Melt the butter and add the sultanas, eggs, sugar and white wine vinegar. Mix well. Pour into the pastry case.
5. Bake for 35 minutes at approximately 180°C/350°F/gas mark 4.

Congregational

Protecting the things you value since 1891

Flapjack

Ingredients

200g margarine

150g soft brown sugar

1 heaped tbsp golden syrup

300g rolled oats

Method

1. Grease a 25x15x2.5cm tin.
2. Melt the margarine, soft brown sugar and syrup together.
3. Add rolled oats and mix well.
4. Turn into tin and bake at 160°C/320°F/gas mark 3 for 25 minutes.

Robert Parkinson, Bath

Fairtrade Chocolate No-Bake Bites

Ingredients

175g Fairtrade organic Brazil nut cookies or digestive biscuits

100g butter

1 tbsp Fairtrade raw cane sugar

1 tbsp Fairtrade golden syrup

1 tbsp Fairtrade organic cocoa

150g Fairtrade sultanas

150g Fairtrade Dark chocolate

Method

1. Crush the biscuits in a bag.
2. Melt together the butter, sugar, syrup and cocoa.
3. Stir in crushed biscuits and sultanas.
4. Press into a 20 x 20cm square tin (or similar).
5. Melt the Fairtrade chocolate and pour over the base when cool.
6. Cut into squares when the chocolate is set.
7. Best stored in a refrigerator, though unlikely to last very long.

Mrs Lyndell Williamson, Huddersfield

Index of recipes

Index of recipes

Index of contributors